SENSUAL MATH

ALICE FULTON

P O E M S

SENSUAL MATH

==

W. W. NORTON & COMPANY
NEW YORK   LONDON

Copyright © 1995 by Alice Fulton

Printed in the United States of America

The text of this book is composed in Centaur Roman with
display set in Adobe Rusticana Roman and Post Antiqua
Composition and manufacturing by Maple-Vail Book Manufacturing Group
Book and jacket design by Hank De Leo
Cover painting is *Sidereal* by Hank De Leo,
39″ × 65″, oil on linen, 1994

First Edition

Library of Congress Cataloging-in-Publication Data

Fulton, Alice
Sensual math / by Alice Fulton.
p.   cm.
I. Title.
PS3556.U515S46   1995
811'.54—dc20   94-32191

ISBN 0-393-03750-9

W.W. Norton & Company, Inc., 500 Fifth Avenue, New York, NY 10110
W.W. Norton & Company, Ltd., 10 Coptic Street, London WC1A 1PU

1 2 3 4 5 6 7 8 9 0

For Hank

CONTENTS

I

II

MY LAST TV CAMPAIGN:
A SEQUENCE

III

IV

GIVE:
A SEQUENCE REIMAGINING
DAPHNE & APOLLO

SENSUAL MATH

I

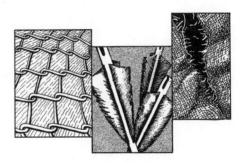

THE PRIMING IS A NEGLIGEE
÷

      between the oils and canvas. Stroke the white
sheath well into the weave. The canvas
needs more veil. The painting
           should float on skins of lead
white coating—or its oils will wither
the linen they touch, its colors gnaw
at cloth until the image hangs on air.
        The canvas needs more veil.

          The body takes its own shade
      with it everywhere. There are true gessoes
         flesh will accept: blocks and screens
to keep the sun just out of reach. Creams
      white as styrofoam but less
perpetual, vanishing like varnish
once they're crammed between the cells.
      So skin is sheltered
         by transparencies, iced
     with positive shadows. Sunshade.
The nihilist is light.
          Printers know it's the leading

between lines that lets them be
swaddled in the rag of stanzas.
How close the letters huddle
     without rubbing. For immersion see

"passion between." See
opposite of serene. For synonym and homonym
see "rapt" and "wrapped."
              There is a gown—that breathes—

and a gown—that heats. One to hold,
                              one to release. Watch
the lead white camisole go up
        in arms and hair and skin.
That one flings it like a shiny jelly
        to the floor. With beautiful frugality, go
the solid cotton briefs.
        The lovers get so excited

to think—nothing comes between them.
                              There is nothing between them.
That's how they can consume each other,
        sand each other sore.
The oils are suspended
        on a leading. The lovers
touch in linen walls.

ABOUT FACE

÷

Because life's too short to blush,
I keep my blood tucked in.
I won't be mortified
by what I drive or the flaccid
vivacity of my last dinner party.
I take my cue from statues posing only
in their shoulder pads of snow: all January
you can see them working on their granite tans.

That I woke at an ungainly hour,
stripped of the merchandise that clothed me,
distilled to pure suchness,
means not enough to anyone for me
to confess. I do not suffer
from the excess of taste
that spells embarrassment:
mothers who find their kids unseemly
in their condom earrings,
girls cringing to think
they could be frumpish as their mothers.
Though the late nonerotic Elvis
in his studded gut of jumpsuit
made everybody squeamish, I admit.
Rule one: the King must not elicit pity.

Was the audience afraid of being tainted
—this might rub off on me—
or were they—surrendering—
what a femme word—feeling
solicitous—glimpsing their fragility
in his reversible purples
and unwholesome goldish chains?

At least embarrassment is not an imitation.
It's intimacy for beginners,
the orgasm no one cares to fake.
I almost admire it. I almost wrote despise.

INDUSTRIAL LACE

÷

The city had such pretty clotheslines.
Women aired their intimate apparel

in the emery haze:
membranes of lingerie—
pearl, ruby, copper slips—
their somehow intestinal quivering in the wind.

And Freihofer's spread the chaste, apron scent
of baking, a sensual net
over a few yards of North Troy.

The city had Niagara
Mohawk bearing down with power and light
and members of the Local
shifting on the line.

They worked on fabrics made from wood and acid,
synthetics that won't vent.

They pieced the tropics into housecoats
when big prints were the rage.
Dacron gardens twisted on the line

over lots of Queen Anne's lace.
Sackdresses dyed the sun
as sun passed through, making a brash stained glass
against the leading of the tenements,

the warehouse holding medical supplies.
I waited for my bus by that window of trusses
in Caucasian beige, trying to forget
the pathological inside.
I was thinking of being alive.

I was waiting to open
the amber envelopes of mail at home.
Just as food service workers, counter women,
maybe my Aunt Fran, waited to undo
their perms from the delicate insect meshes
required by The Board of Health.

Aunt Alice wasn't on this route.
She made brushes and plastics at Tek Hughes—
milk crates of orange
industrial lace
the cartons could drip through.

Once we boarded, the girls from Behr-Manning
put their veins up
and sawed their nails to dust
on files from the plant.
All day, they made abrasives. Garnet paper.
Yes, and rags covered with crushed gems called
garnet cloth.

It was dusk—when aunts and mothers formed
their larval curls
and wrapped their heads in thick brown webs.

It was yesterday—twenty years after
my father's death,
I found something he had kept.
A packet of lightning-

cut sanding discs, still sealed.
I guess he meant to open the finish,
strip the paint stalled on some grain
and groom the primal gold.

The discs are the rough size
of those cookies the franchises call Homestyle
and label Best Before.

The old cellophane was tough.
But I ripped until I touched

their harsh done crust.

A LITTLE HEART TO HEART
WITH THE HORIZON
÷

Go figure—it's a knitting performance every day,
keeping body and clouds together,
the sky grounded. Simulcast, ecumenical
as everywhere, stay and hedge
against the bet of bouffant space,
you're the binding
commitment so worlds won't split.

Last week we had Thanksgiving.
The post-cold warriors held a summit
full of East meets West
high hopes. Why not hold a horizon?
Something on the level, equitable instead.
They said the U.S. Army held rehearsals
on monastic sand. In the desert,
lieutenants zipped in camouflage
thought back to where horizons were
an unmade bed, a nap
on the world's edge.
Privates, nights
when they were sanded
by flower fitted sheets, ground out
in flower fitted skin: her, oh him.

This Michigan is short on mountains,
long on derricks
needlenosing heaven, making evil
electromagnetic fields.
"Talks on the fringes of
the summit could eclipse
the summit itself," the anchor
admitted. Go figure.

Your reticence, your serene
lowness, because of you I have something
in common with something.
Your beauty is *do unto me* and who am I
to put you in the active voice?
I rest my case
in your repose, a balance
beam, point
blank closure
that won't—bows are too ceremonious—

close. You graduate
in lilac noise. You take off
and you last.
You draw all conclusions
and—erasure, auroral—you
come back. But I am here to vanish
after messing up the emptiness.
I am here to stand
for thanks: how it is
given, hope: how it is
raised. I am here to figure
long division—love—
how it is made.

SOME COOL

÷

Animals are the latest decorating craze.
> *This little piggie went to market.*
> *This little piggie stayed home.*
It's a matter of taste.

I have this string of pig lights for the tree.
Each hog is rendered into darlingness,
rendered in the nerve-dense rose
of lips, tongue, palm, sole. Of the inside
of the eyes and nose.
> They wear green bows.

Driving home these bitterly Michigan nights,
I often pass the silver bins of pigs
en route to the packing house. Four tiers to a trailer.
A massive physical wish to live
blasts out the slits
as the intimate winter streams in.
A dumb mammal groan pours out and December pours in
freezing the vestments of their skin
to the metal sides, riddling me
with bleakness as I see it. As I see it,

it's culturally incorrect to think
of this when stringing pig lights on the tree.
It's chronic me.

Our neighbor, who once upon a life
hauled pigs to slaughter,
said they are confined in little iron cribs
from farrowing to finishing.
Said steel yourself
this might be unpoetical and spoke
about electric prods and hooks
pushed into every hole.
About: they cried so much he wore earplugs.

While trimming the tree, I stop to give thanks
for the gifts we've received,
beginning with *Elvis's Favorite Recipes.*
I'd like to try the red-eye gravy—
bacon drippings simmered with black coffee . . .

"Some had heart attacks. Some suffocated
from others stacked on top.
They were pressed in so tight—
hey, what kind of poetry you write? Well.
They suffered rectal prolapse, you could say."

> *Why not spend Christmas with Elvis?*
> *Invite your friends*
> *to bring their special memories of the King.*
> *Put a country ham in the oven and some of his songs—*
> *White Christmas to Blue—*

About: somehow a pig got loose. A sow
fuzzed with white like a soybean's husk.
It was August and she found some cool
under the truck. When he gave her a Fig Newton

her nose was delicacy itself,
ticklish as a lettuce pushed whole into his hand.

Are You Hungry Tonight?
I speak from the country of abundance
curdled brightly in the dark,
where my ethics are squishy as anyone's, I bet.
I'd like to buy the enchanted eggnog fantasies.
Instead I'm rigging the tree with grim epiphanies
and thinking myself sad.

> *For a gut level of comfort,*
> *close your eyes, smell the pork chops frying,*
> *put on "Big Boss Man" and imagine*
> *the King will be coming any minute.*

"At the packing house, some bucked like ponies
when they saw the sun. Some fainted
and lay there grunting to breathe.
Drivers hooked the downers to the winch
and tried to pull them through a squeeze.
Their legs and shoulders tore right off.
You'd see them lying around.
After the showers, they turned a hysterical
raw rose. They shone. The place seemed lit
by two natural lights, coming from the sky and hogs.

Pigs are so emotional. They look at the man
who'll stun them, the man
who'll hang them upside down in chains.
They smell extinction and try to climb
the chute's sides as it moves.

At the top, the captive bolt guy
puts electrodes on their heads
and sends a current through.
I've heard the shock could paralyze
but leave them conscious, hanging
by their hocks from the conveyor
until their throats are slit.
Pigs have an exquisite will to live."

After eight months he quit
and got a job screwing tops on bottles
of Absorbine, Jr.

Now when people ask what kind of poetry I write
I say the poetry of cultural incorrectness—
out of step and—does that help?

I use my head
voice and my chest voice.
I forget voice
and think syntax, trying to add
so many tones to words that words
become a world all by themselves.
I forget syntax
and put some street in it. I write

for the born-again infidels
whose skepticism begins at the soles
of the feet and climbs the body,
nerve by nerve. Sometimes I quote
"At mealtime, come thou hither,
and eat of the bread,

and dip thy morsel in the vinegar."
Sometimes I compose a moaning section,
if only for the pigs.
Like surgeons entering the thoracic cavity—right,
the heart's hot den—
I've heard we could slip
our hands into the sun's corona
and never feel a thing.

ECHO LOCATION

÷

Stop quivering
while I insert straws in your nostrils
and wrap your head in cloth
I have immersed in plaster.
     For a life mask, the subject
must be rubbed with gelatin.
And you must be the love du jour.
     I have studied the duct-taped mullions
of monarch wings for inspiration.
I've learned the paramedic's rip.
          Don't squirm.
(But I ran my finger down its spine
     when its back was turned.)

A perfect containment invites trespass,
          the wish to shave below the skin
     and write in seed ink, *mine.*

     I can testify
the tic of prayer persists in nonbelievers.
     Under my distressed surface, under duct tape,
the Hail Mary has a will of its own.
     The spirit uses me. It holds me up
               to the light like a slide.
It claims a little give, a quiver,

can prevent a quake.
Says copy the vibrato inside trees—
             the star shakes, heart shakes—
        that ruin the wood commercially.
Says you must be ready

      to freeze your extremities
anytime for a better glimpse of the blur.
        Not the blur made firm, mind.
        The blur itself
and not a clearer version of the blur.
        Will you hold it up to the light like a slide?
        Will you pledge your troth
                    and tear this edge off first?

The Norman name for quiver-grass
was *langue de femme.* As in gossip, as in meadows,
        one ripple leads to the next, as in cascade
experiments: one touch and worlds take place.

That's why a little quiver can inscribe a night
                into your left breast,
a day into your right. Can shave below the skin,
        and write in seed ink, *thine.*

But when I think I've ripped the surface
            to the pith, queen substance,
        when I've diagrammed the cry, I

      remember a quiver is a fist
of arrows and the arrows' case, their clothes.
                    Is the weapon and the tremor,

the cause and the effect.
Once the arrow leaves the bow—
                    will-of-its-own-will-of-its-own—
there is no turning back.
       You must be the visceral river.
You must think a little give
       leads to affinities: the arrow
                    resembles the bird it will fly into.

MY LAST TV CAMPAIGN:

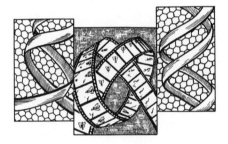

A SEQUENCE

THE PROFIT IN THE SELL

÷

You know that existential twilight
found in rooms lit only by TV?
How the consuming starlight
grinding from the screen will pass
for dusk no matter what
the hour? I ask you. The sun never sets
on "Dynasty." And somewhere
you can bet "Bonanza" 's always
inflicting its tempestuous Western fairy tale
on the air. *Broadcasting.*
It means to throw seeds.

I had retired to find myself
considering the ads I'd written
flashing through every private-
public space in declamatory cascades.
Supplyside, right
brain stuff. IVs to the id and ego.
Get it said and sold with style
in 30 seconds, you get loud fame. A Clio!
High honors for the catchy cobwebs
you sewed in someone's head.
Before being tucked into oblivion,
I wanted to raise something more
than mercenary monuments

to high sales curves.
I'd rather be emerging than retiring. I came out

to sell a big account
that needs to keep its identity
hidden. They're deep
into everything it seems.
A job so sweet you'd do it
for free. Career candy.
I couldn't wish away the rush I felt
once I grasped what they were after:
A campaign that demonstrated the beauty of dissolving
boundaries between yourself and the Martian
at the heart of every war.
An ad that pushed viewers to incorporate-embrace
rather than debase-slash-erase the other
gal-slash-guy. A commercial saying blend,
bend, and blur, folks. It works!
But how to put this spin on their opinion?
How to position—this position?
Advocacy ads are not for beginners.

I was struck by a case history
that was no *once upon a time.*
It really happened, The Discovery
Network said, over some vast stretch.
This orchid fashioned itself
into a female bee, or you
could say, a commercial
for that creature.
By dressing up and passing

as a dummy luscious *she,*
the bee orchid pulled in more
pollinators and survived more

flagrantly. So what, you say. *So what?* So
it was evident. The deep shape of everything is—
transvestism. I know
it's a difficult sell.
Mimicry's a prettier word.
Creation is a form of crossdressing. The ultimate
one-size-fits-all. When he heard, my partner put on

his man-of-the-world-
weary look. "Orchids in drag? Don't make me
laugh." He was ready to throw hooks.
I was ready to throw odes
in the path of flowers
brave enough to reach
beyond their typecasting and accede
to victory. Poets. Or killers.
Good copywriters are either.
If you're both, you get rich.
I wanted to commit sonnets

in honor of these—maximal outsider—carnal flowers
that overstepped their bounds
to complete themselves
with bees. "Complete?" Wilderness
and wing—incessant escalator—dice and fathom
in the stems, the spine's
expansive gossip and
the prophet in the cell—

emerging—coming out,
dispensing with what's stable is what
it's all about. Art, nature, name it,
are fresh recombinations.
My ode goes "Imitation, soul
of innovation! Memory's naught
but summer reruns, reflections
of the sun inverted in the sea." It goes and goes.
As nature knows, it's easier to mix
single-celled existing things
into new and improved blooms
than to build the blossoms straight
from protoplasmic scratch.

When the orchid special ended, I surfed
the channels of hypersmiling families,
steamy crops of frozen foods,
drop-dead erotic cars.
But if television's the common—
village square and looking glass
held up to the big US,
why did I feel sunk
inside the cranial guts
of a machine that made the whole thing up
according to its whim?
I watched that sucker thinking: Its power

is its costume. Its costume
is its *signal*, a trait that changes difference
to affinity. I poked the remote
till my arm felt carbonated, full of Coke,
thinking with the ads
I'd sent thrashing

through their electronic cottages
how I'd inflamed the nation
to spend. I got out my charge
to analyze the charm of its design.
It's the size of holy cards
from childhood, the word
DISCOVER dulled
by the membrane of my prints. The logo's

letters simulate a dawn
or dusk of commerce or wonder—gaining
on the world. What else
to expect from flesh and sense? What rises
more gracefully
to the mercantile occasion or better sets
the earth at rest? Sentenced
to the breakthrough and
dispersal of the day,
the sun does
time and promises. They've made it
the white navel—I notice—in the O.

VANISHING CREAM

÷

TV rules: it must be visual velcro
at four grand per second. Show
them what they've never seen before. Show
the package to change brand preference—show
the product in use. Don't confuse

the consumer. The males prefer dark colors
to light—a velvety surface works better
than a smooth—wasplike shapes
seem more seductive—long and short
hairs should occupy distinctive areas—contrast
spots make dummies more attractive—wait,
those are *orchid* rules. I mixed

a ninety-proof martini
guaranteed to numb me up
and considered how to keep the sizzle
yet let the serious point shine through.

ROUGH SCRIPT OPENS ON
BERT WILLIAMS, THE VAUDEVILLIAN,
DRESSED IN BLACKFACE—hey,
wasn't he black anyway? WIPE
TO TALENT TOWELING BURNT CORK OFF
HIS BROWN-SKINNED FACE. MR. WILLIAMS:

"I DRESSED IN STEP 'N' FETCH IT DRAG
TO PLAY A DARKY ON THE GREAT WHITE WAY."
Most gin is colorless. Sloe gin isn't gin

but a liqueur. You want a cocktail
for the eyes, a flashlight
in their faces, a stun gun
that distracts and seizes, leaving them
transfixed. The time
it takes to be oblique and build
façades that people buy
as slice of life! The straight man
always has less to do. A comedy rule. SWISH-PAN

TO WOMAN IN ORCHID DRESSING GOWN. DOLLY IN
AS FINGERS DART BETWEEN
FACE, FOUNDATION, BLUSH, CONCEALER. WOMAN:
"I'M PUTTING THE RITZ ON FEMALENESS
TO PLAY A LADY TODAY."
I never begin without thinking
this time I'll fail
and be found out. The wares exposed
in calculated volts behind glass screens—TVs
remind me of museum vitrines.
Everything up close. The viewers staring
without daring any hands-on
knowledge. ZIP-PAN.

YOUNG WOMAN PINS NYLONS
TO SHORT CURLY HAIR. MIMICS
IN MIRROR THE TOSSING TURNING
HEADS OF LONG-HAIRED MODELS.

"BOYS REALLY GO FOR THE SILKY STRAIGHT
LOOK." Too little stirring fails to chill or mix
the ingredients; too much melts the ice
and dilutes the kick. VOICE-OVER:
"BLACKS IN BLACKFACE, FEMMES IN FEMMEFACE.
DO YOU KNOW WHERE THE *REAL* YOU IS TONIGHT?"
DISSOLVE. *Dissolve's*

the most beautiful word in broadcasting.
But it wouldn't do. I knew. You know
who wouldn't be enchanted. Besides the client's

vital interests wound up
blurred somehow. My holdings glowed
then vanished in a chorus of bleeps.
Delete. Delete.
Seduced, repelled
by this eclipse, I mixed another,
taking comfort in the ritual
and listening to the audio
leaking from the other
room. SHE: "ANY CHANCE YOU'LL GET SOME
WORK DONE TODAY?" HE: "I'LL DO MY BEST,
BOSS MAN." CUT.

"I CAN'T BELIEVE IT'S NOT BUTTER!"
Double negative. A no-no
going by the rules. "GIVE YOUR SPECIAL SOMEONE
A HEALTHY SQUEEZE." Unflirtatious—
clear and smooth—straight
gin goes down like water. But stir—strain—
add a twist—delicious.

PASSPORT

÷

As an infant, I was kissed by Valentino.
Tango stain and sweat

bouquet of greasepaint—
an unnutritious—foreign taste.
Sandgrains!

The depilatory smell of elegant

black ironed brows—slight needle sticks
from razored cheek—the starry fangs
of slave bracelets and clove

smoke clasped in every fold.

Though I can't say I remember
being only nine months old.

Mother played the Wurlitzer
at local picture shows.

I give you her

rendition. She rose
solemnly from the deep

pumping and pressing
as the giddy instrument
was steeped in sunrise beams

and celluloid reeled

like well-behaved
ticker tape
through the narrow gates.

Her repertoire included STORM FUNERAL
GRUESOME QUIETUDE
THREE KINDS OF LOVE AND

NEUTRAL. But
Valentino—oh—
she wasn't equal

to the moaning hormonal
harmonies he needed. His swagger

rattled her. The six-foot
oasis—liquid

makeup of his face
razed her
to helpless arpeggios.

Our kitchen thickened with stills.

Dad snickered at "The Sex Menace
on the Ice Box." Yet he fretted—

as if secretly crediting
the abductions of swoon

stare and burnoose—
when Rudy bowed

through town. Mother's connections ushered her
backstage and the scale changed

to the minute ahs and ooze
of a connoisseur
as she described the drawing

near. So close
she noticed the recessive
knife tracks in the deadly

jelly of his hair.

He clicked his heels and kissed her
palm, kissed the bald crack

where my skull's plates fused, fixed
or dismissed her
with his desert glance.

In some tellings, she held his hat
as if it might sprout antlers. Yes,
expand into a feral candelabra

while he held me,
reciting poetry

he had composed himself. He sold

Mineralava Beauty Clay
at intermission. Mother said he bungled
the ad by mumbling. Sound was

trauma. He was king of
costume, gesture, the skin

of drama. The erect pinkie

while sipping tea, the kiss he gave his sugar
lump before he slipped it in—

my mother mimicked every move
during bedtime stories.

In a bunting of Boraxed linen, I lay
smoking a thermometer,
listening to plots feverish

with disguise.

The Italian Valentino as an Arab
revealed to be a Scottish Earl—or a Cossack

passing as a bandit
who moonlights as a French tutor.
The Duke of Chartres posing

as the ambassador's barber—or descendant
of the mortal brother of

Krishna reincarnated
as a popular student at Harvard.

Mother recited every subtitle.
They surface sometimes, out of context,
while shaving or passing

the lap-dancing dives
on Seventh Avenue: DON'T BE SILLY MASCHA,
HE'S MASSAGING MY HEADACHE AWAY.

I've seen clips of his astounding dress.
Stitched in little festivals.
His suit of lights in *Blood*

and Sand. Harnessed in
bangles as—*The Young Rajah?* Stripped

to wasp-waist, heart-shaped
beauty marks—hose, wig, garters

as a queen

applies his lips
and simpering lackeys induct him
into lace jabot. A vengeful press

release portrayed him as
"supported by silken pillows,

wickedly smoking sheikishly

perfumed cigarettes."
And a machine dispensing orchid powder

in a men's room led the *Tribune*
to accuse him

of debauching U.S. guys. Right

after this publicity—was I two, three?—
my first memory—Valentino
died. *L'homme fatal.* Of peritonitis.

WILL YOUR MAJESTY KINDLY
SIGN THIS PASSPORT?

The cosmic master-
minds he kept—his spirit guides
and medium in Pasadena—failed

to see his early death. Would he have believed
a greater prophet? Darwin

said agents can improve
their futures without paranormal gurus,
improve by using

environmental feedback: market research.
The sweeps. And Nielsen.

When Rudy passed away, my mother's mind
became an intimate sealed place
my father couldn't fumigate.

Laced in mantillas

as long as she lived
on the day he died

she brought orchids to his crypt
and said her lines: "I am older—

tonight, Master—

but the love is the same . . ."
The tabloids named her
The Lady in Black. Of course,

there were imitations.
One year, five
morbid clones appeared.

But mother was the first. It was her
idea. Her vocation—almost—
you could say. It made her—well—

anonymously famous.

And Valentino was effaced
as consuming passions changed.

Those flappers who found themselves transported
in the dark have died.
Those tie-me-up-

tie-me-down-those-whitely-flashing
eyes! It wasn't the irises
they fetishized.

It was the blanks that sang.

There was music in his reticence
for my mother. And he needed her,

she knew. Without her
what was The Great Lover?
Numb buzz and nuzzling

drone. A face sliding
down an astral shaft—

to mask the screen in dumb expanse.

"WONDER STINGS ME MORE THAN THE BEE"

—EMILY DICKINSON, LETTER #248

÷

1. ELVIS FROM THE WAIST UP

Are you self of my self
or shudder—
alien—other—

the body wants to know.
As for this promiscuous spring
wind, it should be neutered.

I say it should be
fixed—rich as it is
with the invisible invasive

sex lives of the trees.
As for me, I was wheezing
from one faux colonial château

to another on The Showcase of Homes
having laid down my five dollars
to let them try to sell me

a neobaronial heartbreaker
inlaid with wet bar charm. Let me guess
which room's the largest.

No contest. It's the cars'.
The sprightly realtor spots me
for a fellow

connoisseur: "It is evident
the minute you enter
that the interior is

unlike any you've seen."
I want to say "These are the places
that give imitation a bad name."

But knowing what it is
to stand in knotted throat and control
top, with schmoozey syndrome

grins and shakes to sell
the unendurable
durable goods, I say

"No kidding." I praise
the medieval turret *avec* deck.
"It's not fake anything. It's real

Dynel." What did that slogan sell?
Then I cast off
the hospital-issue snoods

they make you wear
over your soles to save
their finished wood.

My body doesn't miss a beat.
It's marshaling its forces
against the goodly grasses.

Mistaking benign outsiders
for low-life viruses. Accusing
the weeds of treason.

I'm sneezing as if I agreed,
though drugs have boned a granite corset
under my relaxed-fit breathing

knits. The immune system's so adept at this
telling self from other stuff
it would reject

a skin graft from a sister, brother.
Heart of my heart,
you go too far, I think as I bless

the inventor of Kleenex.
Who had the greater genius,
the one with the idea

or the one who made us
say the brand name
as we reach? A slowcoach

from the pills, next thing I know
I'm off the map and thirsty
for some liquid summer—

a Sex on the Beach or Fuzzy Navel—
in the inflated meadows
of The Country Club.

My Diet Coke's already poured
when the girl says "I'm sorry.
We only sell to members.

People with accounts."
I'm too put out
to even ask for water.

And returning to my Legend,
a bee flies up and stings me
near my wedding ring.

"... dummies
that engineer a metallic sheen
or add a little glass

are more attractive than actual
females," the orchid show flashed back.
Something about—the bluff,

the Elvis-from-the-waist-up.
"Do you wear falsies?"
a wasted uncle asked

our junior bridesmaid—shaved and teased
to nubile grace—her gown
like egg whites beaten

to a nuptial lace.

2. THE MISSING LINK

I was dabbing on the Afterbite
when this bee got in my bonnet.
Why not say it with flowers?
I lost sight of the golfers
in their clannish plaids

and imagined a long shot:
actors as BEFORE and AFTER orchids.
Men in bee suits buzzing round
on guy wires. A voice-over going
"Welcome to Darwin World,"
and a gent in a frock coat
sewing wings onto a blossom. "Mr. Darwin?

Want the red spots on the petals?"
a lackey asks. Adorable
as hell. The BEFORES
are quintessential wallflowers.
The AFTERS, after Darwin, are seductive—
rushed by bees.
For music, "I Will Survive"
came to mind. Or "How I Got Over."
But no. The Darwin orchid should sing
the old Temptations

song: "I got so much honey,
the bees envy me."
I began by borrowing
slogans from past glories:
"What Good Is Paint,

If It's Not Good Paint"
I dismissed as too cryptic,
"There's Something About Them
You'll Like" as too broad-brush,
"The Dash That Makes The Dish,"
a bit old hat and kitsch.

"Flexible Where You Want It,
Rigid Where You Need It" was too risqué.
Ditto "One Whiff And They're Stiff,"
which some might remember
as the catchphrase for an insect spray.
They might fill in the missing link:
"Quick, Charles, the Flit."

Wheel-spinning, I found a phrase
to speak to their self-interest:
"Discover the Other
Slash You." It even included the second person,
the most exalted pronoun

in the business.
I called my partner on the car phone
and unfolded the idea
with reverent emphasis, dramatic
beats. Ahem. Ahem,
he said. And then
"Who do you think
Darwin was, some 19th-century yenta?"
Was it sexy, would it fly—
these were his criteria
when appraising campaigns
for dog bones or dish soap.

I thought I'd satisfied
both scores. My batting average
assured the ad's survival,
but it didn't stop
the teasing, buzzing
sounds when I walked by.
My cohorts liked to tell jokes.
This one got to me: The BEFORE orchid

is at a carnival with Mr. Bee.
He says, "What would you like to do?"
"I want to get weighed," says the flower.
They find a weight guesser who estimates
two ounces, which happens to be correct.
"What would you like to do next?" says Mr. Bee.
"I want to get weighed," says the BEFORE.
This one's got a screw
loose, the bee thinks,
and takes his crazy date
back to the orchid patch.
"How did it go?" the BEFOREs all chorus.
"Wousy," says the flower.

That's the sensibility
I was up against. This
from those who thought
crossdressing orchids
sounded crass! To show he was no fairy god-
mother to nature's deb ball Cinderellas,
I had the orchids alter their own formals
when Darwin's back was turned.
The talent—discovered in the Rubbermaid
commercial—added stretch to every gesture.

3. VOLUNTEERS

But I remember best the radiance escaping
from the tape as I drove home
each day. Skeins of Bach
crossbreeding in the air.
The instrument's strings
mingling like a chromosome's
toward coronation. Music forming crown
knots and cascades.
To improvise, anticipate and risk—
equilibrium's like kissing

your own hand in comparison.
The first voice gives rise
to volunteers and what a ride!
A feral—formal
congress in the ear.
But evolution is a fugue
without finale. News that stays
news. The road in its unfoldings.
What kept me moving

coffined though I was
in the Legend's leather plush.
Who was I
to try to put new wrinkles
in the sedentary wit of self
and state? I vanquished
Bach sometimes and sang
off key "Wild

Honey," Mozart's Jubilate.
Because the blossoms cannot feel.
That was left for me.

To carpe diem all night long. To think
that for a minute
I made my living marveling
at polyphonic flowers. To think

I was a player.
And at day's end, I was done. So tired
you'd guess I was the shrewd one—God—
who finessed the genetic
legerdemain
and shoved the cell
across the hostile centuries.

WONDER BREAD

*You asked me what my flowers said—then they
were disobedient—I gave them messages.*
—EMILY DICKINSON, LETTER #187

÷

What eucharist of air and bland

was this nation raised on? No one understood
my funny flowers—and Darwin—

Darwin was regarded as a charlatan.
Few viewers think

evolution is the truth.
My flowers *were* absurd.

Snips of sugar. Snails with spice.
Puppy dogs. Tales. Everything.

Nice!

But why did I admire nature so?
Was it that I liked

the absence of a Master
neuron in the brain—

the absence of a Master
cell in embryos—

the nothing in the way of
center that would hold?

What causes less comfort
than wonder?

What—does not console?

III

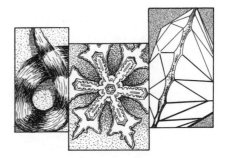

DRILLS

÷

It was one of those summer immersion courses,
where students must speak the language they're learning
in brittle, artificial dialogues,
injecting textbook empathy into the tone:
*"Vous etes souffrant?" "Non, ce n'est pas grave.
C'est le foie, comme toujours."*
A summer so loud with roses
climbing on their little cleats
and sculpting blossoms as they climbed
I couldn't hear myself speak.

Until the teacher plucked me from the chorus
with a question out of sync with all our drills:
"Does suffering help one understand
the suffering of others? What do you think, *Alice?*"
I wanted to describe an essay I'd received—
I also was a teacher—
from a former Marine
who wrote of the wounds, humiliation,
he'd endured in war
and how he'd held up well
until a medic touched him gently.
I wanted to build complex sentences,
quivering with clauses that reveal

the meaning sheath by sheath
and lead to, or perhaps enact, the fact
that understanding is itself unbearable.
Sentences beyond the depth
of my thin French. So I just said yes.

I thought of this
when my sister lost her daughters,
Laura, Marleen,
and no one could fathom how it felt
to build two children from the blossom and pollen
of your body, to breathe
on every detail of their being, and—
no one could imagine.
But I suspected she, their mother, could

understand the stone mason, coaxing so much soul
into a carving that was going
to be an unseen feature
near the spire of a cathedral,
cuddled in the gray immersion
that looks like overness or the smoke
of frankincense, a summary
higher than the eye can see. She might know why

the tightrope artist vibrates between skyscrapers
to link what is forever
separate otherwise,
and how mountain climbers name the hardest routes
since no two calvaries
are quite the same.

In the first twist of grief,
        I saw she could bear anything
            better than a sweetness.
    Certain kindly phrases or embraces
            had the power to dissolve her.
"Don't be nice to me. I can't stand it
            when you're nice to me," she'd say
as understanding drilled into the cell's marrow—
        where nothing had the right
            to ever dwell again.

$$== \\ \div$$

It might mean immersion, that sign
    I've used as title, the sign I call a bride
after the recessive threads in lace==
the stitches forming deferential
        space around the firm design.
        It's the unconsidered

mortar between the silo's bricks==never admired
        when we admire
the holdfast of the tiles (their copper of a robin's
    breast abstracted into flat).

    It's a seam made to show,
the deckle edge==constructivist touch.
    The double equal that's nowhere to be found
      in math. The dash
    to the second power==dash to the max.

It might make visible the acoustic signals
of things about to flame. It might

        let thermal expansion be syntactical. Let it
add stretch

        while staying reticent, unspoken
as a comma. Don't get angry==protest==but a

comma seems so natural, you don't see it
when you read: it's gone to pure
transparency. Yes but.
                    The natural is what

poetry contests. Why else the line==why stanza==why
      meter and the rest. Like wheels on snow

            that leave a wake==that tread in white
                  without dilapidating
                  mystery==hinging
            one phrase to the next==the brides.

Thus wed==the sentence cannot tell
whether it will end or melt or give

      way to the fabulous==the snow that is
the mortar between winter's bricks==the wick that is

            the white between the ink

FUZZY FEELINGS

÷

Is beige a castrate of copper, pink, and taste?
Does lace add blush to any situation?
Do you want novocaine?

I've been staring at the ceiling's
stucco moonstuff for three hours, grateful
for the prickly little star
someone's inked onto a lattice strip.
This light means business, like a xerox

of the sky's allover glow.
I'm seeing nonexistent rainbows
outside, transparency split
into the true colors it hides behind
its see-through guise.

Is the universe an imitation?
Are the cat's tabby cables
a mimicry of snake? How can you tell
a natural emerald from the flux-grown fakes?

Inside it's all beige
partitions, latex gloves, lace tiebacks
and prints of ducks in love.

The drilling decor and rock
make me think I'm in a bodyshop
through which a boudoir's wandered.

Metaphor is pure immersion. Pure sinking
one into another and the more
difference that's dissolved the more==

often I'll sink
into a book that swimless way.
Some volumes turn out to be wallpaper
or boxes for valuables. Simulants

tend to be flawless, while natural
emeralds have defects
known as inclusions, imperfections
with a value all their own.

I'm faking Lamaze and ancient mantras. I'm having
new veneers. The dentist talks about a relative
who boasted over 364 girlfriends
and seduction rooms in every shade.
He was in air conditioning
and smoked himself to death
though he could hold his breath
longer than anyone else.
"My role model," the dentist says.

Do women need fuzzy feelings?
a man asked in the waiting room's
frayed *Glamour*. Do they need simulated intrigue

dinners, candlehours, cuddle-wuddle
teddy bears and wittle tittie tats?
Anything with ribbons on it,
an earthtone rainbow baby angel goose and floral bed.
Do women need texture and men
need sex? "To stick it through
the uprights," this guy said.

Scientists think the universe was smooth before it loomed
itself to a jacquard
of defects known as textures.
A texture is not localized.
It's an overall sensation, like being

enthralled or born, in love or mourning, growing
at the speed of light and leaving
its distinctive signoff on
the sky. Photons—lumps of glow—
gain energy by falling into
a texture after it unwinds.

"I hate rock," the dentist says,
changing the tape for its clone.
What does beige==what does lace==
what does pain imitate? The autopsy
of beige revealed a gelded rainbow,
upwardly mobile ideals. Lace
is a form of filth I hate.
As for the dying moan and gush

of the deer killed by hunters down the road—
I'd find it more tasteful

done in plastic or an acrylic
venison Christmas sweater.
I'd rather wear vinyl than hide.

I didn't mean what I said about lace.
Lace in a vacuum would be okay.
Even beige would have its place. It's context,
culture makes them==wait, I'll take the novocaine.

When I get home, I'll fall into the immense rub
of a robe like a universe unwinding.
I'll talk to Sandy
whose daughter Laura died last year.
(I hate the type's authority in that line, the—
get it in writing.)

When a friend asked how Sand was doing
her husband said "She'll never be the same."
"What a relief it was—to never have to be
the same. I felt so grateful," she explains.
The return to a genuine, originary self
was—thanks very much—not to be

expected. Her imitation would see her through
another evening of held breath.
As we left the "slumber room"
she asked whom Laura most resembled.
I think she==you, I said
in some wrong tense.

Before a party, she blends some body
veil into herself. Gets ready to flex

the verbal abs and delts and hopes
she won't be up till dawn
re-living how she broke into
emotion during her free pose.

Does "grace" mean alive and lucky
to be not writhing?
Or the ability to hide it
when you writhe?
The fissures==vacancies inside

a natural emerald are known as its *jardin.*
I'll leave this place with a refined smile
outside a headache that makes me cry all night.
Right now I'm trying to open wide.

SOUTHBOUND IN A NORTHBOUND LANE

A fetish is a story masquerading as an object.

—ROBERT STOLLER

÷

Her anatomically-correct smile
turned to frown when she turned
upside down: the inflatable naked woman
the student body tossed, cum laude,
through the graduating bleachers.
Like gossip, a bubble bred for turbulence,
         she tumbled
to the Ph.D.'s, who stuffed her
under their seats.
      I think the trick to falling is never landing
      in the palm of someone's hand.
The lyric, which majored in ascent,
is free now to labor and cascade.
What goes up must==
                Waterfalling
means the story visits tributaries
at a distance from itself. Consider
what it takes to get us off
the ground: what engines laying waste
to oil. I'd rather hit the silk
from a span
and let gravity enhance my flight.
Though the aerodynamics of jets are steadystate
and can be calibrated,

I'd rather trust a parachute,
            which exists in flux and can't be touched
by mathematical fixations.
            In what disguise will she arrive—
            whose dissent is imminent yet unscripted—
            offensive as necessary?
            Whose correct context is the sky.
Arrive like something spit out of a prism
in a primary tiger bodice. Be modern
as an electronic vigil light, precisely
delicate as nylon,
the ripstop kind, that withstands
40 pounds of pull per inch.
            Spectators, if we jump together,
            we'll bring the bleachers down.
"I was frightened. My flesh hissed
and I thought I'd perished,
but the sensation of descent vanishes
once the body stops accelerating.
It's astonishing how nothingness
firms up. Air takes on mass.
The transparent turns substantial.
I stretched out on that dense blue bed
until the canopy expanded
like a lung shoved from my body,
plucking me off the nothing matt.
What held me up was hard to glimpse
but intimate as mind or soul.
I sensed it was intensely friendly.
I almost thought it cared for me."
            If you can't love me, let me down gently.
            If you can't love me, don't touch me.
If we descend together

like Olympic skydivers or snowflakes
we can form patterns in freefall.
Like a beeswarm, we can make a brain
outside the body.
When falling is a means of flying,
the technique is to release.

  How many worlds do you want,
  my unpopular bodhisattva?
  Let's sneak one past the culture's
  fearless goalies, be neither one
nor the other, but a third
being, formerly thought *de trop*.
Before I throw my body off, my enemy
of the state, I'm going to kneel
and face the harsh music
that is space.

IMMERSION

÷

Let it be horizon levitating on horizon
with sunrise at the center==
the double equal that means more
than equal to==within.

It's sensual math
and untied railroad tracks==
the ladder of gaps and lace
unlatched. It's staples
in the page and the swimmer's liquid lane.
Those sutures that dissolve into the self.

> Once by night she shoved blunt needles
> through the cotton sheafs. Once.
> By God for the nth time. She'd give
> her stitches extra hiddenness.

Pile dash on dash and stroke the seam-
ripper down the middle.
Let a blank fall down
the posit that never disappears.
If you love the opposite of knot,
the way the center point in shadows can be hot,
let it do what it wants==
to grade the white space like a passing
lane to passing strange.

By night she burned and dodged
to polish up the image.
She agitated paper in three poisonous solutions
until a picture formed.

It's the partly present==that leads the view
out of the frame onto the wall
and lets you finish
the dismembered thing yourself.

Though her day job named bureaucracy
the one infinity
she'd get before she'd get to heaven,
by night she learned a tongue by thinking
only in that tongue. She worked her mind into
its language like the tines of a glove.

So one thought is occluded by another
no less celestial mention in your head==
each sinks in each
as paper can fold back onto itself.
When you unpleat, the crease lingers
and each wing wants to press==consensual==into
the other once again.

By night she sank jewels in immersion cells
to understand them better.
It is a test: when gem and liquid share one
refractive index, a continuum
exists and the solid's limits seem
to vanish. She tried solutions till the stone looked most
completely gone. When there was least gem left,
she could identify it.

Yet immersion's also treason
to a naming that's a nailing down.
It's the barcode riddled down the middle
so the product's up for grabs==
what no register can scan.

     I use it like a comb to unsnarl day
     and sift the blank
     in tones in hopes
     the prism will begin
     its tints in me. Which is to say.
     I'd be close to you as glass is to its double
     glaze and music to its stellar disc.
     I'd be all give. Let me put it like this==

UNWANTING

Laura Fulton Carpenter, 1969–1990
Laura: *Latin feminine of* laurus, *bay laurel*
÷

As the waves grew ample in the outer mantle
of her mind, my mother dreamed
she was at Laura's grave.
There was a picket fence around it,
and inside, a little tree. From each of its leaves
a discrete fragrance reached:
carnation, lilac, rose and more.
She thought—a tree like this will never need flowers.

When she woke, day was undimming
the windows with so much *enough*
that some leaked right into the house.
Over her instant "cup of dust,"
the freeze-dried stuff, and muffin with Promise
that wasn't an abstraction but safflower oil
spread thin, she could still smell
the hardy perfumes—bloom split into bloom's
constituents—within the fence.
She had "Today," her morning shows, the heater
rumbling when she summoned. The touch-tone to me.
But she wanted that tree.

    (To get a grip on memory, hold your hands apart
    like   so
    and think this space, though definite,
    can be minced into ever and much

smaller bits. And staring at that boundlessness
limited by skin, you'll grasp it: things go
farther into diminishment
and still exist.)

I'd like my presence in this hour
to be idolatrous—to have and hold
the instant rather than the else:
the meadows—held by winter purl—and galaxies
of books against the walls.
The synapses of taste, touch, tone
and sight. Of smell—
that helps us know things at a distance.

"I was scared of the fence.
But the tree I just loved.
Where did anybody get a tree like that?"

When the hushed philharmonic of the lightning
bugs upstaged the Independence Day displays,
I realized one firefly—
the minimal—could not have
turned the trees sidereal.
We put out the headlights to take it all in.

Desiring is nothing to having
the night sing to you in scents or gem.
Tree of completion—presence—and immersion,
what can compete with the unwanting—
the exdream—the world gone into god again?

IV

GIVE:

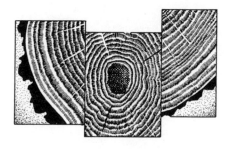

A SEQUENCE
REIMAGINING
DAPHNE & APOLLO

A FOREPLAY

÷

I'll entertain questions before the stellar estrus
        commences: if you want.
                But since it's you I depend on
                to change the lines to living

ground and figure, I'd rather have you
find the answers on your own. Remember how

        music was aroused in the old technology?
The stylus vibrated, shaking a crystal in its head,
        and the groove culled this trembling.
The stylus made electrons fly
        from the atom, climb a wire through
the crystal to the gate. There

        the slight current was amplified,
bridling the large—

        and vinyl gave
rise to sonatas, rise to bop.

        This gives the odd god
and hound dog, dolphin and electron,
        the novation and the moment
of change. Since the truly new
looks truly wrong at first,

it gives the sublime and grotesque,
hoping you'll receive them kindly,
hoping for the best—newness
        being not so much a truth

as it is emotion.
Can you feel for the dark

        matter, background
lines of lace or brides? Will you
        receive the hybridized and recombined,
the downsized and the amplified?

The greenery and systemic herbicide:
        the laurel wreath.

        As estrogenic effects collect—
in heat and blur and curve—will you receive
        the minus and the plus,
the—not to mention, but I must—

        then some inbetween?

MAIL

÷

What they had in common went beyond the I'm-cool-are-you-
cool handshakes and passion
for bloodsport. From forever, they were too alike to get along.
She was incidental
at first, a bit player in their boy-god drama—which began
when each of them
claimed "My Way" as his song. Both were superheroes
in the action-
figure category. Both were fond of cherry bombs. But their
biggest
similarity was this: deep down they were profoundly
superficial.
This kinship prevented them from seeing anything
but difference
in each other's style. Phoebus Apollo favored snapbrim hats,

alligator shoes and sharkskin
suits from Sy Devore's Hollywood men's store. In battle,
stripped to the mail
he wore beneath and crowned with light, he glowed like a
refinery
turning crude into product, roaring Doric columns of flame. "I
make everything
and make it into everything else," he liked to claim. He took
pride

in how cultured he was, a musician of pansexual magnitude
with his suave
ballads of desire. His friends—who had to listen to him

brag
about the last rival he'd skewered against the high F
cymbal,
the broad he'd slammed against a two-way mirror—called him
Your Eminence
to his face and The Monster privately. Of course, he had
his own line
of designer products. His PR people washed the death out of
his image
and got him onto cookies and air fresheners, among other
things.
He could lip-sync in ten languages and was globally marketed
as General Voice
Swoon Pope and Chairman of the Bored, though provincial

to the bone,
he called any place outside Parnassus "Darke County,
Ohio."
Jove was "the Big J"; a good time "a little hey-hey."
Himself he dubbed
The Republic Thunderbolt; Cupid, The Bell Airacobra
Venus Flytrap
and Fluttering Pharmacy of Love—which seems unfair since
Phoebus
gained his own fame as a healer by prescribing Chivas
Regal.

Cupid's skin was napped with floral fuzz and exhibited
a creamish structure,

like mayonnaise but more dense. He resembled a flesh-eating
botanical.
Yet that gosh-darn boyish charm of his made it hard
to credit
the two-shot derringer glued to his thigh. He'd aim
at chandeliers
and light switches, fire into his Ferrari if the battery went
dead.
But his bullets always ricocheted, striking someone
in the heart.
He sleepwalked and needed looking after.
Phoebus
considered him a frivolous child, carney spirit, gyrating
primitive
and part of nature, which only amused the little god.
"I fly
because I take myself so lightly," he'd smile. You'd hear

a helicopter drone.
Then this vision appeared, frosted with glittering filaments
from the soles
of his feet to his little mauve wings—whose nectar-secreting
glands
kept him fat and sticky. Or else it was the fried peanut
butter and banana
sandwiches he always craved. Apollo ate nothing
but pasta
with a dab of porpoise sauce. He despised Cupid for dressing
in a blouse
slashed to the waist and a tiny gold-lined cape from Nudie's
Rodeo Tailors.
For the mixed metaphor of his jumpsuit that flared to wedding

bells white
as a pitcher plant's. Apollo was still exulting over

his recent easy
listening hit when he happened on Cupid's opening
at the Vegas Hilton.
"What right hast thou to sing 'My Way,' thou imbecilic Fanny
Farmer midge larva,
thou sewer-water-spitting gargoyle, rednecked bladderwort,
dirtbag, greasedome
and alleged immortal of a boy," Apollo fumed. "Do thou be
content
to smite the teen queens with thy rancid aphrodisiac and cover
not
my swinging tunes. 'My Way' is my song; with it I have
penetrated
the pestilential coils of rock and roll that smothered
the charts
with plague-engendering form, for which I received
the Presidential
Medal of Freedom and a Ph.D. To think I did all that, and
not like Thor,
and not like Zorro. Oh no. I did much more—" And Cupid
interrupted, "Your way

is all head and no heart. I'll get you cock-cold, you technical
reptile.
I'll neuter you, dude. I'll delete-obscene-verb your brains
till they bleed.
When the King's feeling vengeful, this old world sees stars.
He holds
his crossbow like a Fender guitar. He makes
a hybrid

from a dog and a god. Their hearts go WOOF when he shoots
his wad."
So saying he twitched his wings and flew directly to
The Aladdin Hotel in Vegas.

There he pressed two records of opposite effect: one fostered
an autonomy unravished
as the winter wind's; one, an imperial grunt, made the listener
wish
to dominate and call it love. The first, unlabeled, went to
Daphne,
who adored the wilderness between territory and names.
The other,
on the SUN label, was mailed off to Apollo who mistook it
for a tribute
from his star cult and was pierced. Cupid hadn't forgotten
how Apollo
thee-and-thoued him. He gave the God of Truth new words.
"Well, strike me pink,
what a fix I'm in," Phoebus found himself saying.
"I'm belching
like the hound that got into the gin. Pard' me for trying to
give trees a hug.
I'm in love. Umm! I might throw up." Daphne,
meanwhile,
began stockpiling weapons, studying strategic arms in friendly
competition

with Apollo's sister Phoebe. Like Phoebus, Phoebe loved
a fast bird,
a good gun and same-sex parties. Each member of her all-girl
band

had a signature whistle the others used as summons.
Daphne
swirled with them through the forest, neither mortal nor
immortal,
but a creature inbetween. Her beauty was mutable.
Take
her hair, redly restless as a vixen's or dolphin-
silver
from minute to minute. Frothing like white water it was
channeled
by a single ribbon so tributaries escaped and trickled down her
face. A dangerous
draw followed in her wake. Downstream, her current seemed
friendly, ready
to negotiate and give. Upstream you had to fight the deep
meanders of her
mind. Many wanted her and how to coax a river daughter

from her chosen
bed became the question. She would not
be dammed.
Hissing, camouflaged by a palladium haze, she'd bounce
sound
off distant objects to predict their motion, shape, and place.
Echolocation
is what she used to navigate, traveling up to one hundred miles
a day.
Her sonar let her see right through opacities: read
the entrails
coiled inside the trees. The skeletons of beasts looked
lightning-struck
to her: locked in the moment when the bones glow
through

the skin, and given three outwardly kind people, she could find the one
whose heart was sour. But her gift for visualizing the inner

chambers
of words was most impressive. She'd tell of *wedlock's* wall
that was a shroud
of pink, its wall that was a picket fence, the one of chainlink
and one
that was all strings. While Apollo hardened with love for her,
Daphne
stripped the euphemism from the pith. *Love* was nothing
but a suite
of polished steel: mirrors breeding mirrors in successions
of forever, his
name amplified through sons of sons and coats of arms,
her limbs
spidering, her mind changed to moss and symbol, a trousseau
of fumed wood,
the scent of perforations as his relief rose above her
smokey field.

THE LINES ARE WOUND ON WOODEN
BOBBINS, FORMERLY BONES
÷

A daughter like the openwork of lace==between
the raised motif

the field, formed by lines
of thread called brides, shies back

in order to let shine. The design
from negative space

shapes its figured river==suns
star==the white thorns==sperm==and patterns

verb the ground. Through the brides'
or pearl-ties'

airy flesh of net, wayward electrons
spin

with their absent grace and
windowing

through the opaque==the dense
omissions crystallize the lack

that's lace. She is to be that
yin of linen

that dissolves
under vision's dominion==be the ground

of silk that's burned away with lye==
the bride.

TAKE: A ROMAN WEDDING

*... She, hating the whitethorn wedding torch
as if it were a thing of evil ...*
—OVID'S METAMORPHOSES, BOOK I

÷

It was lit at the bride's hearth while she played
    at resistance, clinging to her mother's arms
        in lovely terror: let me be chaste! Her part
        in the mock rape was to beg.

A parade formed to take her
                to his house.
    What festive obscenities.
                She listened.
    Pipes and timbrels.
                Venereal hymns.
    Thigh or breast?
                What wild X is seized?

The groom tossed walnuts like a soiled confetti.
    A boy ran with the torch. A portent.
                If it soared: children.
                If it flickered: a jinx.
The orange veil hid the right of her glance.

            It was a drastic enhancer, the fire
thrashing round the whitethorn core. It was hair
        grabbed by heaven, coronary-colored. Spires
from Apollo's crown, it gored the night. Spermed

a tail like a comet's
                    and metastasized
to her new hearth.
                    Became
        a tossed bouquet.
                    Became
heavier on consummation,
            when the smoke was weighed.

The remnants, a negative
                    of baby's breath,
were divided by the guests.

Once upon a bride there was a time.
Between twelve and twenty. But a minor

        all her life. Once—no often, every war—
    she was taken by force, as spoils, as lifting
                    her over

the threshold remembers.
                    And the whitethorn still grows.
The organza branches

                of today's hybrids—though susceptible
                    to fireblight—
            are entirely free
of nettles.

UNDOING

÷

Take:
her wish to be chaste. And exist in violent cloister.
To be unravished as a prime
of rainbow—a red or blue
unsplittable
through any prism. Take
the as-it-is-as-it-is—
the script. Use two hands and twist.

If you're a virgin, what are you doing
running around the woods, getting raped?
Curving every which way
in nonconjugal space.
Don't you know the best manners are the least
obtrusive? Your presence pursues its own undoing.
Just asking for it: Just use two hands and twist.
As it is as it is: your femaleness naturally
says take. Says this rape has your name on it.
Your beauty provokes
its own dominion, whose no can never mean no.
How does that one go? TO OPEN
SCRIPT PUSH DOWN WHILE TURNING.

While spinning her negative charge
she has—like a wave—no single location.

If pushed through a slot, her velocity
compounds. Take
a hue outside the spectrum,
an unchromatic octave
higher than the eye can see,
a singular—unravished shade. Name it she.
Her color, name it nevergreen.

As to her bareness and her glance,
he wants to array it in flame
sandals and flame veil, a white tunic
with a double-knotted sash.
Give it an iron ring.
Put on its high-heeled sneakers—put
its wig-hat on its head. Its dress
of a fine smooth textile
made in filament and staple form
from wood pulp
solutions extruded through
spinnerets
and solidified in baths or air.

He wants to part her hair with a lance.
To make her rayon likeness,
evergreen as glance. His composite
new improved her. Cast her
in fibers of modified wood pulp found in
butcher linen or tire cords.

Prestige involves accumulation.
His desire to collect her
assumes a type—and others of the.

A kind—not one of a.
A whole forest to be had.
Let arrows stand for probabilities.

If he bored in close he'd find her bare
charge higher than it seemed==an infinite
beneath an infinite shield==an infinite
that can't be split
by modifying in the middle.
Neither soft nor hard, dull nor
bright, she traveled fast and had no given.
The more he tied her down as to position
the less he knew of her
momentum. Always transported, always elsewhere
before he==*who was she*

to tabernacle in the woods?
Place a minus sign in front of it.
Haze her
escape. TO OPEN—LINE UP ARROW
ON SCRIPT AND VICTIM
PUSH SCRIPT UP WITH THUMB.

No matter how many of her he gathered together
in his name, she would not
be the natural he could cultivate.
Though cast as lady or grotesque,
as hectic membrane in the flesh,
she would be neither-nor.

SPLICE: A GROTESQUE

÷

(DAPHNE)

From un-image, a form sexes itself to presence, gaining ground
    and traction, draws itself
                together, erect
in chlorophyll surround and flapping like the sun
            up close, like a raptor, becomes
the popular god, the can-you-imagine rose and thorn
    under wraps, the classical glance of him
      visible for an instant as he
ripples between stills, trying to settle
    into his perfection like a nest,
                trying to light,
to don his marble artifice, flare into
        his precise foreverness.

Pulse. What use is that to him. Go figure.
    Given the heavens, he's the stellar,
not the black bridle between stars. He's the type
    on white, he's text. He's monarch, please,
he's god. The impressive==living end.
Though luminous matter is less than one percent
      of the whole
required for closure, though foreground
was an afterthought, he's the great attractor the field falls
    on its knees before. Go figure.
When he speaks his subjects

want to listen up—be liked
by such exclusionary beauty. Oh please.

And trying to introduce himself and light,
trying to settle his perfection like a net,
to produce his sovereignty, I.D., he's taken aback
by what's recorded
in the velour ground of his voice,

and I witness, riveted,
as he naturalizes, looking surprised,
as his suede bass mutates—
"I pray thee"
blurring to "Hey Baby,"
"Ah me!"
to "No sirree!"
Witness as he yields his definition,
shrinks, grows
jowls, pants, bays,

drools like a hound, all his torch
pulled downward—is transposed
from lyric plea to what my mother called dog minor,
and his scent—the exsanguinated scent
of godly flesh—the rank smell
of hound begins to foul it,
surprising him, still clinging to eminence
as he naturalizes, pure splice,

hymn to hound—raptor to roadrunner—blurring
before firming up—

as witness, I am midwife
to the pulse, the composite
pelt and feathers, the nascent maybe
monstrous innovation of
a god with a gift in his teeth,
who bows
until his mouth is thrust between his legs,
wags his tail and stammers—
"Hey Talltits, I ain't stealing what you own"—
and I realize he thinks that—
"Just a bit-a bit-a honey
that you have on loan"—what I'm living in,
the dark matter of myself—
is his.

÷   ÷   ÷   ÷   ÷

My mother's thistled lyrics
whiptail into mind.
I witnessed as she sang herself
into top billing at The Apollo,

upstaging everyone with her seminal presence,
using her unretractable claws
to form and deform oracles, her songs
to open cyclone fencing,
gnaw through planks and deadfalls,

voice to drag a live
trap chained to massive logs, climb the walls
and splinter bars—saw the mainstream

call her marginal, though she was a star
in her own field, big enough
to give the spotlight to her backup band,
say "Play your solo, honey,"

before shouting her hit,
the one that didn't crossover
but made the King rich
in his cover version,
say—"Now I'm gone

to do my *own* self song" and sing
the lyrics he'd omitted—
"Want to steal my power, want to steal
my soul—you ain't lookin' for a woman,
you is lookin' for a hole—"

lines that stem through me
as Phoebus tries to urge her from my head—
to drown, femme, wrestle—
what verb—god—
yes, god her saurian voice into the ground.

÷   ÷   ÷   ÷   ÷

Give again the legend
that her tongue bore a charge
and could be used as a support,
how she'd eat her own skin to keep elusive,
how she was something

nothing could stalk,
give her unscannable—knowing

hunters wait for the quarry to step forward
she'd stay withdrawn, the planet—
Big Mama, Gaea, Earth Goddess—
underneath their stance,

give her command to turn—turn—

the story of her death,
how she was embodied as the python—dragonlady—
till something struck her—clamped on—
her voice was bathed in exaltation—
till something clamped onto her like—Apollo

who'd built a ring of thorns
around her as she slept—
so that trying to escape, she was impaled
on the barbed crown—Apollo—

who crept within the mantic embers of her death
to steal the oracle—boasting
that he'd killed the monster==this god of light
who wants me
to love or pity him, I cannot
tell, he's that grotesque==god who threatens

"You can lose a bay leaf
from a laurel tree—lose-a lose-a your lunch, dear—
but you'll never lose me, uh-uh-uh—
no siree," defends
"Doggone it, Bachelor-Girl, I'm Phoebus not a fibber,
so be a Natural-Girl,
not a hairy Ladies-Libber," sweet-talks

"Inky-Dink Nymphie, don't say toodle-loo—
          I'm Apollo, not some moron out to oo-
                    oo-oogle you," wheedles
"Yo! Miss Daphne, doncha say amscray—
          How 'bout it baby,
                    wanna hear 'My Way?' " flatters
"You're a real sharp article,
          and I want you for my steady—
don't be a frigid particle,
          say all right already," a god who chatters
"Listen little lady, you're mighty pretty scenery
          but if you don't get friendly,
                    Pops will turn you into greenery—"
snapping his fingers, rhyming "bimbo" with "limbo—"

because light is a bully,
          shoving everything it touches—
                    existing to figure
                    pattern and scheme
          rather than let things rest

in the nocturnal recessed bed==

$$\div \quad \div \quad \div \quad \div \quad \div$$

He told her he was high class,
          but she could see through that.

Chanting her labels—
          Backbeat Baytone Broom Arhoolie
          Peacock Pointer Solid Smoke Buddah,

her albums—*Jail* through *Stronger Than Dirt,*

        I skirt the limits of detectability,
become the knit and backbone of immersion
        against which everything exists—

become the skin under the gooseflesh—in her words—
        I lense, I nevergreen—

        I dedicate myself to reticence,
                and blending ahead
of the high-octane god—
                whistling by above his range—
    "My heart is barking" I hear him pant
    and have to laugh—I hear the thing

she always said when I attended
        her immense voice in my head—

she, whose buried teeth could sprout an army,
     (do girl)
who lived in her luxurious revolving hut,
     (do girl oh)
her agon of corrosion and sowing,
     (do remember me)
chemise of moss and rust,

              I hear her grandly in my head—
commanding honey—I want you to. She wants me to

turn.

Into what, I always wondered—

Turn.   Into the huge nocturnal
      noose around the Virgo cluster?

Turn.   She never finished the sentence—

      till now—I hear her asking me at last to

Turn—her—loose—

SUPERNAL
÷

Apollo pulls a cloud back like a foreskin
              on the sky that is his body.
His laserscope will amplify
              the available starlight,
zero in on the nymph
      in her stealth boots
              that leave no helpful scent.
Daphne—who is graphite,
      darkling, carbon as the crow—

                       is out of breath.
If only the stars would tire,
      she might find cover.
If only they would empathize.
      But who will help a person
      on the wrong side of a god?
All largo, she turns to face Apollo.

Though she expected him
              to wear blaze orange, supernal
as the sun, he tracked her down in camo-
      skin, which "disappears in a wide variety of terrains."
He owns every pattern in the catalogue.
      After considering *Hollywood Treestand*
           ("all a nymph sees is limbs")
      and *Universal Bark*

("a look most guys relate to")
he chose a suit of *Laurel Ghost*
printed with a 3-D photo of the forest,
                which "makes you so invisible
        only the oaks will know you're there."
Even his arrow's shaft is camo.
        Only his ammo jackets gleam
                like lipstick tubes.

Is it any wonder, when his wheel-bow
        has been torture-tested
to a million flexes,

                his capsicum fogger
fires clouds that can cause blindness,
                his subminiature heat detector
finds the game by the game's own radiation,
                and the tiny boom mike in his ear
lets him hear a nymph's grunt from 200 yards—

any wonder—when the ad said
                "Put this baby to your eye
and see if she's worth harvesting" and
        "See the hairs on a nymph's ass,
                up close and personal"—
that he turns the housing, gets her
        on the zeroing grid,
and now his snout at her fair loins doth snatch?

Who can she turn to, the monastic, almost
                abstract Daphne?
The stars are tireless. She decides—
        no, winds up—
        pleading, in extremis, with her father:

"... I am not like
them, indefatigable, but if you are a god you will
not discriminate against me. Yet—if you may fulfill
none but prayers dressed
as gifts in return for your gifts—disregard the request."

That's when her father makes her
into nature, the famous green novation.
And Daphne—who was hunter and electron—
is done with aspiration.
Did you see it coming? You're a better man than she.
With no one to turn to—
she turns to a tree.

TURN: A VERSION

÷

(TREE)

She'll get out of this one somehow. Someday she'll break
our engagement
with a wraparound roll-off or axel full twist
dismount,
followed by a blast of wind that puts an end to this
grotesque togetherness.
"The suckers love a weird wedding." That's what
her father said when
she called on him for help. Forget Io and Arachne. He was
thinking Teenage Mutant
Ninja Turtles. Roger Rabbit, Mr. Ed. People get a kick
out of ambivalent
betrothals and collisions full of give. Flowers that
remodel
themselves to look like bees are nice, but the scientist whose
atoms get commingled
with a fly's might be my favorite. "Help me! Help me!"
I can identify.

Yes, it tamed her, being changed into a tree, but consider
what went
on in me. I had a moment's prodrome, the premonition
before seizure or disease.
I heard voices—"Hi, I'll be your server for tonight" and
"Can I see your I.D.?"

Then in a migraine pink epiphany, I knew I was
a tree. "It"
turned to "me." As Daphne sank, ensorcelled by my thorazine
hush, I heard the
whitewater rush of what I was. To you it might have seemed
"the tree heaved upwards
and twisted like a sleeper in brown sheets" but the process
felt plaid
to me, like madras bleeding—color stabbing color

as it never does
in nature. Heavenly hurt. I recognized the presence
of design.
She moved through my zen nap like a queen—
yes Your Deviance—
riding up like a skirt, abrading my chambers and rays till she
crowned. Oh,
she was a sensation. It was not consensual, let me tell you.
Whose "no"
can never mean "no"? I was opened and she was spiralbound
as nature/culture,
the great divide, broke down. "I'd like you to meet Daphne,"

said the River God, her father.
Please—what's the word for opposite of—"like to meet
Daphne?"
What's the word for what is doing ground loops, flying
the great circle course,
uppity, aspiring, reaching 100 knots in me?
Daphne apparently
did not know her position. I experienced tremendous
interference.

She said she was changing to nighttime frequency: it was dark as a casket where
she was headed. "What is your position?" I transmitted. "Partly cloudy,"
she responded. "What is your position?" I asked again. "Approximate.
Whistling now. Please take bearing on us and report..."
"We are unable...
it is impractical to take a bearing on your voice," I said. "We are circling...
must be on you but cannot see you," she came through. I felt the lead tickle of her

ribbons, her heavy mittens with a trigger finger stitched in, her nuclear skirts and
coppertoed fauve boots. She was carrying an old Kentucky rifle, a Pioneer
Drift Indicator and a "very orange kite." "I'm dead meat,
she said, and then—"I am not friendly." That must be when I freaked. I drooled
amber as trees do when they're hurt. I salivated resin blond
as baby shampoo, lactated the bud-gold of extra-virgin
olive oil to trap the pathogen, Daphne, in a gown of sap for good.
What's the phrase that means how fast the growth layers spin? Velocity of
domain. I circled her in no time, head to toe, in a million wedding rings.

My first emotion happened to be revulsion: an ungreen, sour
cramp
as Daphne shrank—"oh baby," he kept saying—from
Apollo's colonizing kiss.
Of course, he liked her better as a tree. "Girls *are* trees"
was his belief. Mediated
forms pleased him. "If you can't find a partner, use
a wooden chair,"
he'd say. Well, every fetish tells a story. I felt her bows
and powders,
guns and arrows change to pom-poms, a cheerleader's pleated
skirt.
"As she jumps up try to pull her to the sky and slightly
forward," he coached.
"Every beat in a yell should have a motion. Give us an A,
Give
us a P! End the yell with a good freeze." Then her power
mount pike
through—she tried to get away—became
a shoulder straddle
to cradle—as "Nice Save!"—I caught her in her grave.
I choked
on volts of hairspray as—step-step-step-ball-
change—
she became his pep club. Pure as a
symbol,

toned, in racing trim, for her just standing still was grim.
"Safe
in your alabaster chambers," she'd sigh. I noticed she became
more babyish

as the centuries passed by. She couldn't walk, had no control
over her body,
and often babbled rather than talked: "Sis-boom-bah. Doobie-
doobie-doo.
Oo boy or oo girl?" Frivolous. Gerber's gibberish.
And I
became her pacifier. She called me Mr. Crib.

Oblique
grain develops after an injury—like Daphne
teething
on my rings. The growth tornadoes, polarity
breaks
and the grain departs from the ideal of straight==deviating==
making waves
that form diverse and beautiful chambers. People find it
hard
to say which way a tree is spiraling—whether dextral or
sinistral—
and mistakes are often made. The Germans say with or
against the sun,

the English, clockwise or counter, from the on-high
perspective of the gods.
In America, the vortex is described by observers
on the ground, with much
twisting of wrists and waving of arms. But no one sees it
from the standpoint
of a tree. Oblique grain is useless for transmission
poles, plywood, or veneers,
and so a tree with it is thought abnormal: a "monstrositat."
But spirality

isn't a sickness or condition. Since it makes me less desirable
to commerce
and being harvested is not in my best interests, I consider it
a plus.

I had zero spiral before Daphne. I've heard the aberration
depends
on what it turns against. And every part of me has turned
against
a woman's body. The stretchmarks *she* developed are a story
in themselves.
We talked by thought which made us really close.
Others
might consider her a kvetch, but we became best friends.
I understood
because I *was* her by then, wrapped up in the electric flex
of her
ideas: I learned women were debarred from sweating and
vision seeking,
that the female was the prey of the species . . . adapted
to the egg's needs
rather than her own. When Daphne first heard this she'd
begged her father,
saying "Feed me, also, River God,
lest by diminished vitality and abated
vigilance, I become food for crocodiles—for that quicksand
of gluttony, which is legion. It is there—close at hand—
    on either side
    of me." He agreed but later, of course, he changed

her to a tree. To me
she was unnatural. People don't realize—"natural"

is a habit.
Once otherness gets in, a something else entirely begins.
Newness
isn't truth so much as a motion. At first, I resented her
efforts
to transcend me. It was like sleeping with a jostled beehive
in my stem, between her
vengeful "next times" and torrential "should-have-dones."

I said
"You should have sought your *mother's* help when trying to
escape."
But face it, mothers were the ones who bound their
daughters'
feet. The experts said deflate him with a spike heel or a hat
pin, but
who wears such things? Not *this* wood nymph. And he was
a god,
for Christ's sake! He had all the stellar leverage. He was a
tactician
of infinity—a god! Her mother, Gaea, was the Earth Goddess,
yes—
but she'd always pressured Daphne to major in Home Ec.
"Man produces, woman
reproduces." Her mother took that line. "Why can't you
be a gatherer
like all the other girls?" "Next time I'll go for the less

embedded delicacies," Daphne cried. "I'll mime 'little'
with my index
finger and thumb." I'll say this: she wasn't a pleaser.
She lacked

a slave mentality, though she modeled herself on Apollo's
twin and "modeled"
is probably too weak a word. She *did* Phoebe. She had a
Phoebe act.
It was Phoebe this and Phoebe that. She ran with Phoebe's
band and cut
quite a figure as The Little Sureshot Riverbrat, Maid of the
Myth, with a star
on her hat. She could snuff a burning candle with a bullet,
break
five eggs before they hit the ground and pierce the ace
of hearts.
All with her back to the target, while aiming in her compact.

When captured,
she kept shooting through my cambium, reaching beyond
the bodycast
of lassos I'd become, and her hand, part of her hand, her
trigger finger
I think, got slammed outside my trunk and is preserved there
in amber, an organic gem.
If brass were clear, it would resemble amber. If wood were.
Silk as flesh
kept always clothed, gold as cologne, as beer, as urine, warm
to the touch,
absorbent, *elektron* in Greek or substance of the sun, light
in the fist,

amber—collects a negative charge when rubbed. It preserves
organic tissue
very well, which might explain why Chopin handled
amber chains

before performing and Roman soldiers wore amber-studded mail

as their palladium. I was surprised to find 200 terms for it in certain

Polish dialects. But no word exists that is the opposite of "like to meet Daphne."

The more private the wish the less likely there's a term

for it. Did I say she's always having visions, as in ancient versions

of the myth? She sees herself discovered, maybe

in my side,

washed out of context, or buried in blue earth. She'll tell her story

rather than be held inside its web. There are holes— have you noticed—

where the seams don't quite close? Daphne peers through those gaps. She

scans the sky and plans to stare—you can almost hear her glance—

down the air, the blank, the optical until

a face stares back.

STEREO

÷

(TREE)

A sea pen, these mirrors, the lively gray
of oceans with the ocean's active, turnstile look.

The god, wanting to placate her, implanted these
to make the cage of me seem larger.
Now she who was so eager
for a view, a glimpse of the remembered

weather, sloshes up
against herself in silverface
on every side.

"I think that I shall never see . . ."

She seems perplexed at being her own tether.
I hear her say it is yourself you

do this to, I am like you, and wonder who
is being accused.

"If a mirror starts to fall,
let it. Never try to catch it."
A caution

I recall as again, again,
against the self of her that he installed
she hurls herself—

        so entertainingly—

who could bear to save her.

A NEW RELEASE

÷

(DAPHNE)

A voice changed to a vinyl disc, a black larynx,
spun
on the hi-fi as we called it, before light was used to
amplify
and the laser's little wand got rid of hiss. The
diamond-tipped
stylus stroked the spiral groove and guitars flared out of
reticence:
the first bars of a hit. I always wanted to hear it
again,
though it was always in my head: sticky,
invasive,
and what else in that culture was that
dark?

Easing the new release from its sleeve, I saw myself
bent
out of shape in its reflections: a night whirlpool or a
geisha's
sleek chignon, an obsidian never reached by skin
since skin
always has a warmth of blood beneath. It was a synthetic
Goodyear black,
like all records, pressed with a tread the needle traced,
threading

sound through ear and nerves and marrow. I touched its subtle
grain sometimes wondering how music lurked in negative space
that looked so unassuming. The marvel was—the missing had volition.
And the spaces between tracks were a still profounder black: darker than bitter-
sweet Nestlés, coffee ground from chicory, or Coke. Black as it must be inside

a tree. "Wear My Ring Around Your Neck," the latest hoodlum Cupid sang.
He aimed at objects and hit people, it was rumored.
His urgent nonsense—
about hound dogs, rabbits, class and lies—changed
aren't to *ain't*,
were to *was*, *anything* to *nothing*. "Caught" was the operative verb.
While couples jived and twisted I must have listened differently—
as to a special pressing—with my head against
the set. Somehow, by the last chill tingle of the cymbal I wanted
to be the singer rather than the wearer of the ring.
To this day,
rodents gnawing at the wooden walls remind me of the rasp

of dust
before a cut. A cut. That's what we called a song.
And handsaws—

harvesting the forest in the distance where I live—
sound
like the end: the rhythmic scribble of stylus against
label
when everybody's left. Everybody's gone
to bed.
And the record turns and turns into
the night.

WITHOUT WHICH

"Passport": Page 37, "I am older—tonight, Master—" is quoted from Emily Dickinson's letter #233.

"Supernal": Page 99, the quote beginning "... I am not like / them, indefatigable ..." is excerpted from "Feed Me, Also, River God" by Marianne Moore, published in *The Egoist*, III, August 1916, and uncollected since. I'm grateful to Cristanne Miller for bringing this poem to my attention.

"Turn: A Version": Pages 101–102, the dialogue quoted in the stanza beginning "said the River God, her father" is excerpted from *The Sound of Wings: The Life of Amelia Earhart*, by Mary S. Lovell.

Page 103, stanza two, lines two and three: the quote is from Emily Dickinson's poem #216.

Page 105, stanza two, the quote is from "Feed Me, Also, River God," by Marianne Moore, first published in *The Egoist*, III, August 1916, and since uncollected.

ACKNOWLEDGMENTS

The American Voice: "A Foreplay"; "Mail"; "The Lines Are Wound
    On Wooden Bobbins, Formerly Bones"; "A New Release"
Chelsea: "About Face"; "Immersion"
Chicago Review: "Fuzzy Feelings"
Epoch: "Unwanting" (in an earlier version)
Kenyon Review: "Drills"; "Echo Location"
The New Yorker: "Industrial Lace"; "Some Cool" (in a somewhat
    different version)
Parnassus: "My Last TV Campaign"
Pequod: "Undoing"; "Splice: A Grotesque"; "Supernal"
Ploughshares: "A Little Heart To Heart With The Horizon"
Postmodern Culture: "=="; "Southbound In A Northbound Lane"
Southwest Review: "The Priming Is A Negligee"
TriQuarterly: "Take: A Roman Wedding"; "Turn: A Version";
    "Stereo"

"Give:" A Sequence Reimagining Daphne & Apollo also appears
in *After Ovid: New Metamorphoses* (Faber and Faber, London; Farrar,
Straus & Giroux, New York).

"A Little Heart To Heart With The Horizon" appeared in *Best
American Poems, 1992; Poems for a Small Planet: Contemporary American
Nature Poetry;* and *Cape Discovery: The Provincetown Fine Arts Work Cen-
ter Anthology.*

"The Priming Is A Negligee" appeared in *Best American Poems,
1994,* and was awarded the 1993 Elizabeth Matchett Stover Award
from *The Southwest Review.*

I'm very grateful to the John D. and Catherine T. MacArthur
Foundation for a fellowship that allowed me to write these poems.
I also thank The University of Michigan for a sabbatical leave.
Warm thanks to Jill Bialosky for her help in shaping this book:
above and beyond.